Jim Henson's™ LABYRINTH™

BESTIARY

BESTIARY

Illustrated by

Iris Compiet

Foreword by
Toby Froud

Written by
S. T. Bende

THE JIM HENSON COMPANY

LONDON

An Insight Editions Book

CONTENTS

FOREWORD
BY TOBY FROUD

I started out life within the Labyrinth, and every once in a while, I enjoy going back. Playing baby Toby, I was stolen by the Goblin King and taken to his castle. It was up to my sister, Sarah, to journey through a magical world full of strange creatures and unlikely friends to save me and, more importantly, find strength and courage within herself. This is where my love of *Labyrinth* began, and like many new generations who have since discovered the film, my love of *Labyrinth* continues to this day.

That world was brought to life by the stunning designs of Brian Froud and the magic of the Jim Henson Company.

I grew up in the "real" world, surrounded, inspired, and loving the truly astounding and magical work of my father, Brian, and mother, Wendy Froud, who was a creature workshop artist on the film. The artwork they have created throughout the years has continually inspired generations of fans around the world to not only believe, but also become artists and creatives themselves.

As artists, Brian and Wendy create their work using a fine balance of fantasy and reality. It leaps off of the page at you, and their three-dimensional figures draw you even further into amazing worlds. Their work truly breathes life into fantasy and makes the viewer long for other worlds just beyond reach— not only the one seen in *Labyrinth*, but also many more beyond.

It has always been an honor to meet new and wonderful artists who have been inspired by my parents' work—people who have taken that spark and, using their own talents, have made worlds and creations that they then bring to new audiences and generations.

Iris Compiet is certainly one of those amazing artists whose images draw the viewer in and allow them to see beings of whom we can only dream and long to have in our reality. Iris, like my father, does this with great mastery of the pencil and brush, creating images that stimulate and stir the senses and allow you to be taken along on an otherworldly journey.

The Labyrinth is a place where goblins roam and magic is found. What was created and brought to the screen by Brian Froud and Jim Henson has now been enhanced and brought forward by Iris Compiet in this book. Her work invites the next generation to explore these pages, where they will find new and exciting creatures, as well as beloved friends.

"Should you need us," Sarah's friends told her at the end of the film—well, within these pages is where you will find them all, whenever you wish to journey back to the center of the Labyrinth.

THE WORLD OF THE LABYRINTH

Mysterious, magical, and delightfully disconcerting, the world of the Labyrinth is made up of wide-ranging landscapes and uniquely diverse creatures. Ivy-covered walls, odorous bogs, and dark winding tunnels are populated by a plethora of protectors. Each creature strives to prevent visitors from reaching the heart of the maze, where the castle of the Goblin King casts its ominous shadow. It is from within that fortress that Jareth controls every corner of his kingdom, molding time, space, and even gravity to his unique sensibilities. The land of the Labyrinth is thus a beautifully uncommon—and highly unpredictable—realm.

The outermost levels of the Labyrinth emit an aura of calm. Here, the topography consists of a tree-lined countryside, with gently rolling hills and the occasional blooming bush. But just beyond this quiet reprieve lies a chaotic realm. For within the Labyrinth there exists a seemingly endless series of walls, barriers, and obstacles. These obstructions are designed to disorient adventurers and force wayward travelers to abandon their quests. Those who manage to overcome the barricades will discover a myriad of environments unlike any seen in the natural world. From the revolting Bog of Eternal Stench to the seemingly peaceful forest of the Fireys, the regions of the Labyrinth are as diverse as their inhabitants. And among those residents, perhaps none is quite so unusual as the Goblin King himself.

As monarch, Jareth controls the fates of all who live within his realm. He sits within his spiked and spired castle, commanding a network of spies from atop his elegant bone-backed throne. His many subjects—from the simple lichen to an unwitting dwarf—inform their ruler of all that takes place within his domain. Those who displease him may find themselves suspended atop the Bog of Eternal Stench or cast into a role of eternal servitude.

Although the Goblin King's mastery of the elements make him a formidable monarch, he is not the first to govern this land. Legend has it that years before Jareth first served as ruler, the great Owl King oversaw the wilds of the Labyrinth. It is said that he established many of the territory's customs, from the employment of spies to the law that any deal struck may also be unstruck. In tales of his dynasty, fairies, merfolk, wererats, and satyrs lived alongside heroic worms, valiant bandits, and a cowardly bush with a noble heart. Each of these creatures was careful to steer clear of the Owl King's intimidating enforcers—the fierce Featherfang and the terrifying night troll, Septimus.

Though time has passed, the Labyrinth's unique topography, rare flora, and curious creatures have remained staples of a land that continues to fascinate residents and adventurers alike. While little is known about many of the Labyrinth's inhabitants, each deserves our wonder, deference, and regard. For although we may never fully understand their remarkable existence, we can surely learn from their unique traits and behaviors—just as we can learn from the Labyrinth that shaped them.

Overview of the Labyrinth

The Outside

Just outside the Labyrinth sits a vast valley—one rimmed by tree-laden hills and stark brambly bushes. An antique clock bearing thirteen hour markers sits atop a barren tree, while the Goblin King takes to the skies in the form of an owl, keeping careful watch over his landscape. A sharply winding path leads into the valley, where rocks, shrubs, and a handful of flowers conceal a variety of winged creatures. Larks sing overhead, and fairies dart between bluebells, taking shelter in their delicate blossoms.

The Entryway

The outermost wall of the Labyrinth is marked by a thick wooden gate. Cracked vines and pale blossoms cloak the barrier's beams. And just beyond its heavy doors, a thick mist conceals high bricked walls. The walls' dark stones are broken up by barren branches and leafless boughs, creating a corridor that seems cold and unwelcoming. But a closer inspection reveals an array of beasts thriving among the bricks—including a handful of intrepid allies.

The Labyrinth

Beyond the entryway rests the maze itself. Here, among a bounty of dusty-brown bricks, live the subterranean Brick-Keepers. These high-strung creatures manipulate the pathway's stones and yell at anyone who dares to disturb them. Deeper into the maze, the Four Guards, a quartet of canine-like creatures, stand before a set of doors. These guards protect two distinct passageways—one that will guide travelers to the castle at the center of the Labyrinth, and another that will lead to certain death.

The Oubliette

On the opposite side of the guarded twin doors sits a cavernous hole—one that descends to a deep dark shaft. The walls of this cylinder are wreathed with the Helping Hands—curious creatures that guide visitors toward their desired destination. These amenable and enthusiastic hands use both shapes and words to communicate their query to travelers. Would they prefer to go up or down? Those who elect to pass down through the shaft are deposited into an oubliette—a desolate stone cavern that serves as a holding cell for anyone the Goblin King wishes to forget.

The Underground

Just outside the oubliette, resting directly beneath the maze itself, a sea of dark stone tunnels hosts a deceitful troop of troublemakers. These False Alarms misdirect passersby, inaccurately informing visitors that they have stumbled off course. A deeper journey into the stony hallways uncovers rocks, cobwebs, and the clanging metallic cutters of a chilling contraption. Goblin Cleaners pilot this multibladed device as it barrels through the tunnels, removing any debris—and lifeforms—from its path.

Above Ground

Above the underground's exit rests a light airy landscape. It is here, set within a beatific sculpture garden, that the Wiseman dwells. This cryptic sage offers guidance to passersby, while his birdlike Hat interjects with comments of his own. Nearby, goblin guards patrol the area on reptilian steeds. And thick hedges, green vines, and a wide leafy tree lead to the thick wooden gate that houses the Door Knockers. These contentious metal creatures have the power to grant access to the treacherous territories that lie on the other side of their doors.

The Firey Forest

Ferns, trees, and cobwebbed branches frame the entry to the forest standing just beyond the Door Knockers' gate. Sparkling shrubs reflect the dim light of the woods, disguising a number of traps and hidden tunnels. This misty, swamp-like terrain supports a multitude of lifeforms, including the wildly fierce Fireys. These playful creatures are among the Labyrinth's more resilient residents. Unfortunately, they fail to grasp the fact that human limbs are not quite as malleable as their own.

The Bog of Eternal Stench

Beneath the walls of the Labyrinth sits a perilous—and putrid—swamp. With its moss-cloaked branches and repulsive odor, the Bog of Eternal Stench is the Labyrinth's most foul-smelling region. Merely touching its water will cause a passerby to reek for the remainder of their life. Although such an environment may seem uninhabitable, the noble knight, Sir Didymus, finds the air to be sweet and fragrant. He makes his home in the Bog of Eternal Stench, alongside his faithful steed, Ambrosius. These champions watch over the bog's lone bridge, ensuring that no one crosses it without their permission.

THE JUNKYARD

With rolling hills of junk, as far as the eye can see, the region at the edge of the Goblin City houses a peculiar breed of beings. Junk People roam cluttered hills in search of treasure, carrying their finds in piles atop their backs. Though this region is considered unlivable by many of the Labyrinth's residents, it harbors a series of rooms used by the Goblin King to prevent travelers from infiltrating the Goblin City. Within these hidden cells, visitors are trapped in a fabrication of their own lives—a distraction that causes some to forget about their mission. They may be surrounded by familiar objects and engaged in beloved hobbies, but their home within the Junkyard is just a shell of their former reality.

THE GOBLIN CITY

At the edge of the Junkyard, double gates mark the entrance to the Goblin City. A sluggish, aging goblin guards the first of these gates, while the imposing behemoth Humongous mans the second. This goblin-controlled robotic sentry deters most trespassers from entering, but those who successfully bypass him will discover the winding cobblestone streets and densely packed stone slab structures of the Goblin City. Cats, mice, and a collection of chickens roam these roads and winged beasts with long legs soar across the sky. Although much of the city has fallen into disrepair, it provides a safe haven for many of the Labyrinth's goblin residents.

THE CASTLE

The castle at the heart of the Labyrinth is dark, cluttered, and beset by cobwebs. Despite its opulent architecture, the Goblin King's home is overrun with his untidy underlings. These goblins circle wildly around Jareth's throne, leaving food, garbage, and chaos in their wake. Although the castle has many open spaces, other areas are eccentrically cluttered. At the whim of its owner, the castle's structure can shift into a multitude of forms, proving once again that the Goblin King controls everything within his kingdom.

VISITORS TO THE LABYRINTH

SARAH WILLIAMS

Teenager Sarah Williams is a dreamer. A creative girl with an impressive imagination, she is thoroughly immersed in her own universe of make-believe. When Sarah isn't reading plays or rehearsing lines from whimsical plays, she's decorating her bedroom so it aligns with her vision of a fair and fantastical world. Stuffed animals—including her beloved teddy bear, Sir Lancelot—costumes, and her prized music box are artfully placed to reflect Sarah's fanciful ideals. But it is this same sense of whimsy that causes Sarah such struggle. For while she would happily spend all of her hours dreaming, she is forced to contend with the occasional responsibility—such disappointments leading her to reach out to the unlikeliest of allies.

When Sarah is asked to babysit her baby brother, Toby, the infant cries so loudly that Sarah begs the Goblin King to take him away. But when Jareth does what Sarah asks, the shell-shocked girl demands that he release Toby at once. The enterprising monarch then negotiates a deal. If Sarah can reach his castle before the magical clock strikes thirteen, he'll allow her to take Toby home. But if Sarah fails to navigate the Labyrinth, her baby brother will be forced to remain with the goblins forever. As Jareth disappears, Sarah rushes bravely into the Labyrinth. She's determined to save Toby—and she doesn't have a moment to lose.

Sarah's sense of wonder serves her well within the maze. Her familiarity with fantastical worlds ensures that she takes the Labyrinth's unconventional encounters in her stride. And her willingness to suspend disbelief allows her to uncover walls, loopholes, and opportunities that others might miss. Sarah is comparatively fragile in a world of aggressive fairies, fiery foes, and the all-seeing Goblin King. But her determination, and her love for Toby, see her through the Labyrinth's multitude of challenges. After all, the maze reflects Sarah's personal experiences. And through a series of arduous trials, it helps her develop her own unique strengths.

Within the confines of the Labyrinth, Sarah is cut off from her everyday world. Gone are the chores, curfews, and day-to-day responsibilities. But in their place lies a momentously crucial duty—saving her infant brother from the clutches of the Goblin King. Through her adventures with the noble Sir Didymus, his faithful steed, Ambrosius, and the gentle giant, Ludo, Sarah discovers the value of teamwork. In bargaining with the obstinate dwarf, Hoggle, she learns that life is not always fair. Through her confrontation with the Fireys, Sarah uncovers her own strength. And when faced with the loss of her brother, Sarah realizes that she doesn't truly want to be alone. As she soon discovers, sometimes a single selfless act can lead to a wealth of self-discovery. In her journey along the Labyrinth's winding roads, Sarah learns that growing up doesn't require her to leave her childhood behind. Rather, she can carry pieces of her journey along with her and put them to use in new and imaginative ways.

TOBY WILLIAMS

As the apple of his parents' eyes, Sarah's cherubic baby brother lives
a charmed life—or so his sister believes. But when Toby is captured by
the Goblin King, he's ripped from the world he knows and thrust into one
where creatures, goblins, and a highly erratic monarch live side by side
in a chaos-filled castle. Despite the madness that surrounds him, Toby
eventually adjusts to his new environment. In fact, he comes to view the
goblins and their king as amusing entities—rather than the threats that
his sister knows them to be.

MERLIN

Sarah's faithful furry friend, Merlin, accompanies her on countless quests. From adventures through town to dramatic performances in the park, Merlin is Sarah's constant companion. The shaggy sheepdog's amiable disposition makes him a favorable foil for his owner's theatrics. And his optimistic approach ensures he never complains, even when Sarah races home in the rain and denies him entry to the warm, dry house. The loyal Merlin will always show up for his humans— wherever they may need him.

ADVENTURERS OF THE LABYRINTH

Despite its magic—or perhaps, because of it—the Labyrinth can be an intimidating place. Many of its residents toil in deliberate obscurity, keeping their heads down to avoid the wrath of the Goblin King. But a select handful are born great, achieved greatness, or had greatness unwittingly forced upon them.

While each of the Labyrinth's adventurers come to their roles in distinctly different ways, in the end, they form friendships that change not only their own lives, but the very fabric of the Labyrinth itself.

LUDO

Loyal, strong, and fiercely protective, Ludo stands by his allies in good times and bad. This devoted companion escorts Sarah through her trials within the Labyrinth—seeing her safely through the Bog of Eternal Stench and protecting her from the perils of the Goblin City. The rusty-haired creature doesn't shrink from the Goblin King's threats. Rather, he declares his fealty to his friends and fights for their freedom. Through his steadfast commitment, Ludo shows his companions that he will support them through any ordeal—no matter how dangerous.

Though his fearsome growl frightens many a goblin, it is Ludo's gentle nature that sets him apart from the Labyrinth's multitude of beasts. Beneath his fierce exterior lies a kindly creature—one who proudly bequeaths those he deems worthy with the most noble title of all: "friend."

With his imposing size, thick horns, and resonant roar, the hulking creature emits an air of danger. But Ludo's gentle disposition and his lumbering gait make him a target for mischief-making goblins. As a result, Ludo has developed unique ways to protect himself from the Labyrinth's many dangers.

Among his varied defenses, Ludo possesses the power to summon rocks. They gather at his bidding, providing an array of projectiles that he can launch at his opponents, or becoming stony footholds that he can build into a bridge. These tools are Ludo's most formidable defenses, and he uses them to protect his beloved friends.

HOGGLE

When Sarah first meets Hoggle, the brusque dwarf with a penchant for solitude is under the employ of the Goblin King. As a result, he repeatedly turns his back on the girl—and even conspires against her. But as the hours tick by, the normally paranoid dwarf becomes a reluctant champion and true friend to Sarah. And when she needs him most, Hoggle summons his strength and rushes to her aid. In time, Hoggle comes to believe that he may not be destined for a life of solitude, and that, maybe one day, he might just be free of the Goblin King's command.

Hoggle is a bipedal humanoid being with a bulbous nose and protruding ears. He has a fondness for shiny objects, and proudly wears the plastic bracelet that Sarah offers as a gift. His diminutive stature leaves him at a disadvantage when facing more substantial creatures. To compensate, he's honed a strong survival instinct—one that drives him to act in his own best interest.

Indeed, Hoggle has endured the Labyrinth's many trials by keeping his head down. But he also aligns himself with dynamic allies, from the brave Sarah to the all-powerful Goblin King.

Hoggle's lack of athleticism and his desire to avoid conflict suggest he may never become the fiercest of fighters. But his ever-softening heart and growing sense of loyalty make him an advantageous accomplice for any visitor to the Labyrinth.

SIR DIDYMUS AND AMBROSIUS

Jovial, brave, and blessed with an overabundance of confidence, Sir Didymus protects the bridge across the infamous Bog of Eternal Stench. None may pass without his permission, and he screens potential pedestrians with the utmost scrutiny. Though his ego is rather inflated and his mannerisms over-the-top, both Didymus and his steed, Ambrosius, guard their province with great tenacity and honor.

With his long-whiskered eyebrows and spindly limbs, Sir Didymus is a most peculiar creature. His body is covered in fur, but he walks on two legs and dresses in fanciful attire—the pants, jerkin, and feathered cap of a medieval knight. He also wields a staff, both to protect himself from assault and to punctuate his many statements. And he bends a bowlegged knee whenever he meets a damsel. Unbeknownst to him, Sir Didymus's sense of smell has been horribly compromised. He is blissfully unaware that the bog he guards carries a terrible stench!

Sir Didymus considers himself the most valiant knight in the land—and he'll fight anyone who tells him otherwise. When squaring off against the imposing Ludo, he refuses to cede to the much stronger creature. Rather, he carries out his duty to defend the bog's bridge with a gallant—though unintentionally amusing—air. His word is his bond, and he considers valor to be the utmost of honors. And although he follows a strict moral code, Sir Didymus discovers there is some wiggle room in his duties. His new friends can be allowed to pass over the bridge—as soon as he grants them permission!

Ambrosius, a fainthearted sheepdog with a fondness for flight, is the first to run from any sign of trouble. But despite his timid nature, Ambrosius is the most devoted of comrades. He bears a striking resemblance to Sarah's canine companion, Merlin, and happily serves as Sir Didymus's faithful steed. While his sense of self-preservation is strong, Ambrosius is fiercely loyal to his master—a trait that frequently lands him in perilous predicaments.

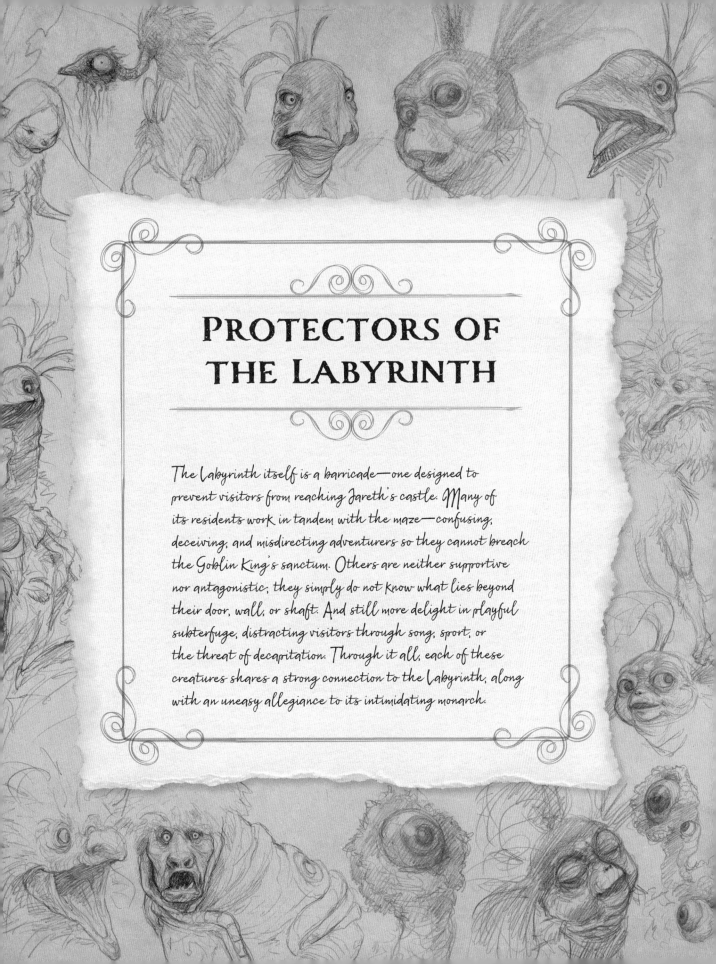

PROTECTORS OF THE LABYRINTH

The Labyrinth itself is a barricade—one designed to prevent visitors from reaching Jareth's castle. Many of its residents work in tandem with the maze—confusing, deceiving, and misdirecting adventurers so they cannot breach the Goblin King's sanctum. Others are neither supportive nor antagonistic; they simply do not know what lies beyond their door, wall, or shaft. And still more delight in playful subterfuge, distracting visitors through song, sport, or the threat of decapitation. Through it all, each of these creatures shares a strong connection to the Labyrinth, along with an uneasy allegiance to its intimidating monarch.

FAIRIES

With their lithe willowy bodies and smartly shimmering wings, the fairies of the Labyrinth bear a sharp resemblance to those in Sarah's storybooks. But any similarity to these fairytale creatures ends there. The fairies of the Labyrinth are far from friendly and have no intention of granting wishes. Rather, they are prone to fits of violence, often biting the fingers of even the most well-intentioned stranger. Because of this behavior, fairies are frequently seen as pests that require extermination.

Fairies seek protection in bluebells, ducking in and out of these blooming bulbs and concealing their bodies beneath the soft petals. Their silent flight enables them to elude predators, while their sharp fangs provide a secondary means of protection.

THE WORM

Some of the Labyrinth's most curious creatures are among the most difficult to locate. Nestled atop a low brick ledge, the cheerful Worm stands ready to assist. With his tufted blue hair and his crisp red scarf, the Worm greets visitors with a hearty "Allo!" His warm demeanor makes him a charming conversationalist—one who will happily invite a stranger to come inside, meet the Missus, and stay for a nice cup of tea.

And while his sage counsel may help newcomers to identify the Labyrinth's hidden doorways, this creature is just as likely to inadvertently lead an adventurer away from her destination.

Living within the Labyrinth's walls, the comfort-loving Worm and his Missus are kindly allies to those who need them, readily sharing all that they have with their guests.

THE FOUR GUARDS

Positioned before a pair of twin doors, the Four Guards are as confounding as they are peculiar. Guarding the left door are Alph and Jim—two dog-like creatures that stand on bowed legs. The pair wields a single shield, which is decorated with an array of runic carvings. Alph stands atop his upside-down counterpart, bantering joyfully with both Jim and the two guards positioned beside them.

Ralph and Tim oversee the right door. Their blue attire complements the paint on their shield and distinguishes them from their crimson-cloaked neighbors.

As upper guards, both Alph and Ralph live by a rigid set of rules—they are allowed to answer visitors' questions, provided an inquiry is posed to only one of these watchmen. The guards must also answer all queries in a specific way—one shall always tell the truth, while the other will always lie. Although none of the Four Guards offers any direct answers, a well-posed question can yield useful information. If phrased correctly, the right query might even help a traveler journey safely through the Labyrinth!

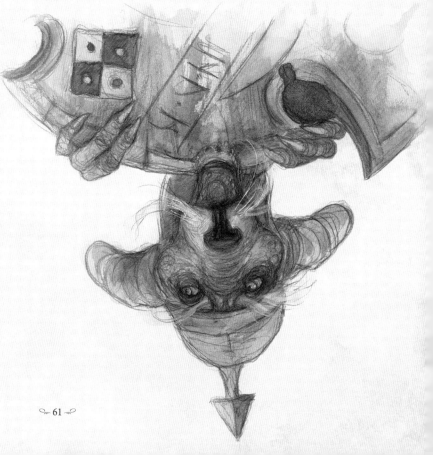

THE HELPING HANDS

Lining the walls of a dark narrow shaft, an assemblage of hands grabs at anyone traveling down their cylindrical corridor. At first, these creatures appear alarmingly aggressive. But once they've gotten a sense of their guest, they are ready to be of assistance—a trait befitting their name. The Helping Hands communicate by forming themselves into faces. Fingers take the shapes of noses and brows, offering expressive reactions to a visitor's inquiries. At the same time, thumbs morph into makeshift lips, raising and lowering in time with their hands' declarations. This combination makes it appear that the hands are speaking through their finger-mouths—a sight that is mildly unsettling, though certainly in keeping with the Labyrinth's sense of peculiarity.

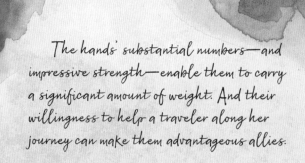

The hands' substantial numbers—and impressive strength—enable them to carry a significant amount of weight. And their willingness to help a traveler along her journey can make them advantageous allies.

THE FALSE ALARMS

The False Alarms are carved stone faces with deep resonant voices. They take pride in erroneously announcing that a visitor has lost their way. But those who hear these misleading warnings should take heart—this attempted diversion means that a traveler is actually on the correct path!

THE WISEMAN AND THE HAT

Nestled within the hedge-lined sculpture garden lives a wise old man and his sentient bird-headed hat. Sitting comfortably atop their stone throne, they rest among a maze of airy green shrubs. There, the Wiseman contemplates thoughts of unfathomable depth, while the avian Hat squawks a myriad of insults. Though their relationship is contentious, the two will gladly counsel those who seek them out—although they might ask for a contribution in exchange for their advice.

Because the Wiseman has accrued decades of wisdom, he is able to offer insight that is both practical and astute. He knows that the way forward is sometimes the way back, and that quite often it seems like we're not getting anywhere when, in fact, we are. And he teaches Sarah one of the most important lessons of the Labyrinth: All is not always what it seems.

Perched atop the Wiseman's head, the Hat interrupts, criticizes, and irritates his owner. His long neck and elevated placement give the Hat a lofty perspective—not only on the world around him, but also on the unusual man upon whose head he makes his home. Although the Hat often feels slighted, he is fiercely protective of the Wiseman. It is the Hat who ensures that no one disturbs his companion's meditative moments and who collects the tribute for the Wiseman's prudent counsel.

THE BRICK-KEEPERS

These subterranean creatures live beneath the bricks that make up the Labyrinth's confounding pathways—and take great offense should anyone disturb them. The Brick-Keepers walk on two legs and have long arms, sharp voices, and wild frizzy hair. Wearing elaborately embroidered garments sewn from fine materials, they slink about the Labyrinth, careful to hide from passersby.

When a Brick-Keeper's path is upturned—or
even just drawn upon by an artistically inclined
traveler—it angrily reorients the stones so as to
discourage further vandalism. Short of temper and
gifted in verbosity, the vigilant Brick-Keepers
always make their feelings known.

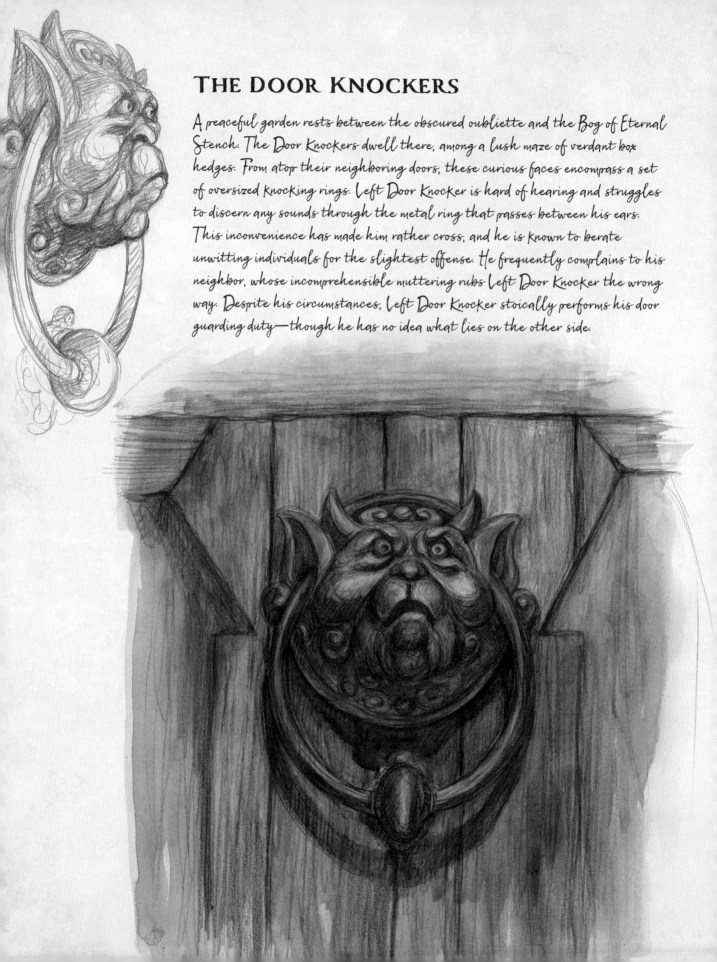

THE DOOR KNOCKERS

A peaceful garden rests between the obscured oubliette and the Bog of Eternal Stench. The Door Knockers dwell there, among a lush maze of verdant box hedges. From atop their neighboring doors, these curious faces encompass a set of oversized knocking rings. Left Door Knocker is hard of hearing and struggles to discern any sounds through the metal ring that passes between his ears. This inconvenience has made him rather cross, and he is known to berate unwitting individuals for the slightest offense. He frequently complains to his neighbor, whose incomprehensible muttering rubs Left Door Knocker the wrong way. Despite his circumstances, Left Door Knocker stoically performs his door guarding duty—though he has no idea what lies on the other side.

From his perch atop his thick wooden door, Right Door Knocker fires off mumbled retorts. Largely unintelligible owing to the enormous ring wedged into his mouth, Right Door Knocker's counsel is often misunderstood. His contentious relationship with his crotchety counterpart makes conversation difficult. But it is his timeless advice, "Knock and the door will open," that ultimately guides Sarah deeper into the Labyrinth.

THE FIREYS

Enthusiastic, excitable, and just the slightest bit unhinged, the brightly colored Fireys thrive on chaos. These good-natured troublemakers seek fun in any form, greeting visitors to their forest with exuberant laughter. When asked, they will cheerfully disclose their desire to have a good time. However, anyone averse to combustion, disorder, and the possibility of dismemberment is advised to steer clear of their revelry.

The Fireys are two-legged creatures with long arms and dexterous fingers. When struck against a rugged surface, the tips of their digits erupt in a blaze. This ability, paired with their layers of flame-hued fur, lends the Fireys their apt name. Their coats stretch from torso to head, leaving the Fireys' legs and arms bare—and thereby less likely to erupt when hit with errant sparks. Expressive ears reflect these creatures' moods, flexing and flopping in time with their owners' fervor. The Fireys use their long tails for balance and often incorporate them into their dynamic dancing. Due to their intrinsic sense of rhythm, the Fireys are frequently found tapping out tempos on a wide range of objects.

Perhaps the Labyrinth's most malleable beasts, the Fireys have the unique ability to detach segments of their bodies. Limbs, heads, and eyeballs can easily be removed without lasting repercussions. Reattachment is a straightforward process—one need simply pop a leg or head back into place! Firey eyeballs, however, must be swallowed whole before they can be returned to their sockets.

The Fireys are communal creatures. They live in family units, or Fire Gangs, and work together to fulfill their life's purpose of having fun. The Fireys find amusement in the simple things, from games of kick-the-head to the rearranging of body parts. Although their social structure appears to be lawless, the Fireys actually live by a hard-and-fast rule: "You're only allowed to throw your own head."

SWAMP CREATURES

These slow-moving creatures flit about their home in the Bog of Eternal Stench. They live in the foliage alongside the marsh, where they build nests from reeds and errant twigs. Their long necks and sharp beaks give them a birdlike appearance, and they peck viciously at anything that remotely resembles a berry. Swamp creatures use their dexterous hands to snatch aquatic bugs from just below the water's surface. But all swamp creatures know that if they linger too long, they might be ensnared by one of the region's many predators—including the long-snouted fish that leap from the water to swallow prey whole!

SWAMP SPIDERS

These four-legged critters, with their confoundingly curious eyes, scuttle about the Bog of Eternal Stench. They spin their webs among the plant-lined banks and feed off tiny insects that frequent the watering holes. Though they may look friendly, they carry a sharp bite—one that causes their victims to swell, itch, and in some cases, dissolve into fits of hysterics.

THE EYE LICHEN

Interspersed throughout the Labyrinth are the Eye Lichen. These keenly observant creatures watch over the maze, carefully studying everything around them and reporting their findings back to the king. They alert Jareth when travelers bypass an obstruction, and they warn him when a resident is working against his best interests. The Eye Lichen grow on the walls of the maze itself. These curious creatures use their multiple vantage points to observe all, making themselves indispensable to their monarch.

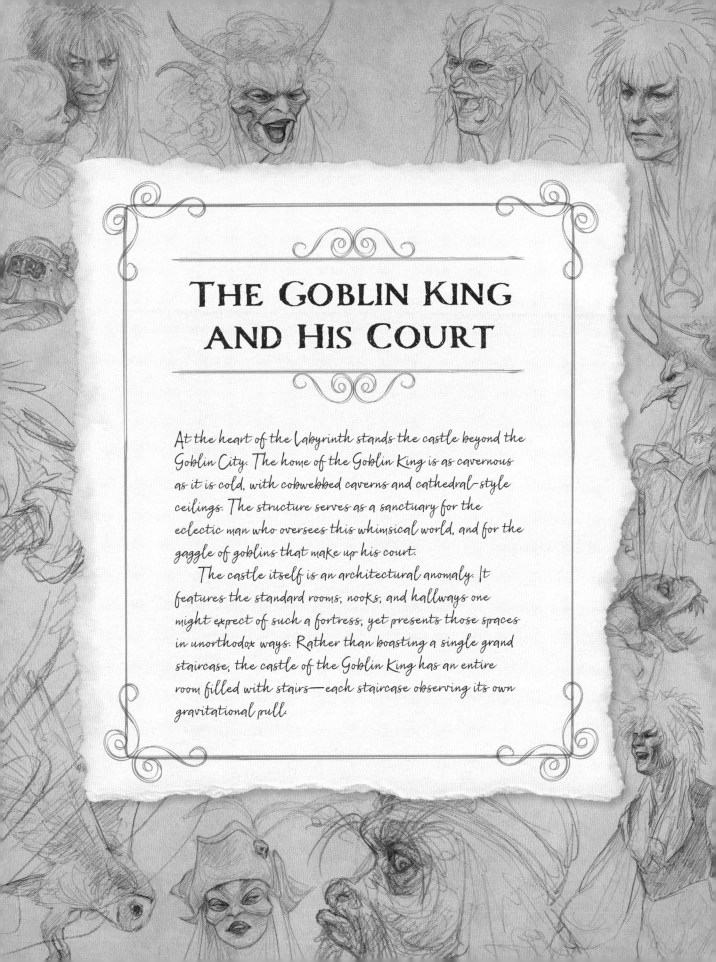

THE GOBLIN KING AND HIS COURT

At the heart of the Labyrinth stands the castle beyond the Goblin City. The home of the Goblin King is as cavernous as it is cold, with cobwebbed caverns and cathedral-style ceilings. The structure serves as a sanctuary for the eclectic man who oversees this whimsical world, and for the gaggle of goblins that make up his court.

The castle itself is an architectural anomaly. It features the standard rooms, nooks, and hallways one might expect of such a fortress, yet presents those spaces in unorthodox ways. Rather than boasting a single grand staircase, the castle of the Goblin King has an entire room filled with stairs—each staircase observing its own gravitational pull.

JARETH, THE GOBLIN KING

The Goblin King rules from atop his curved throne, overseeing his minions with barely contained disdain. The goblins within Jareth's court serve a multitude of functions: preparing meals, protecting the castle, and offering their ruler diversions from the onerous task of governing. Those who have earned the Goblin King's favor are entrusted with prized positions—from serving as valet to escorting important guests. Though easily distracted, the members of the court remain ravenous in their desire to appease their master.

The Goblin King is a masterful manipulator. When he captures the infant Toby, he knows that Sarah will follow her brother into the Labyrinth. Jareth then draws on his multitude of disguises, deceptions, and illusions to ensure that the siblings remain trapped within the maze. Despite his solitary nature, Jareth hopes that Toby might succeed him to the throne—and that Sarah will remain with him as a pivotal part of his world.

Jareth's fixation with Toby is rooted in his own childhood. The Goblin King is said to have arrived in the Labyrinth as a baby—an intended heir to his predecessor's reign. Jareth sees similar potential in Toby and works tirelessly to prevent Sarah from rescuing her brother. Although Jareth delegates many of the more banal childcare duties to his fawning goblins, he delights in entertaining Toby with singing, dancing, and the magical crystalline orbs he uses to observe both the Labyrinth and the human world.

Jareth is an accomplished shape-shifter. He
frequently transforms into a white owl—a configuration
that offers him an alternative means of observing his
kingdom. In this form, Jareth soars high above the
Labyrinth, watching with a calculating eye to ensure
all is as it should be. He also enters Sarah's
world as an owl, keeping himself hidden while
he watches over her.

Beyond his ability to shift shapes, Jareth has a strong aptitude for disguise. When spying within the Labyrinth, he drapes himself in rags and takes the form of a beaked beggar. In his effort to enchant Sarah, he masquerades as an elegant prince. Jareth's uncanny ability to transform himself through a variety of means allows him to manipulate every situation. He molds himself into characters who are uniquely constructed for each circumstance and enable him to coerce those around him to bend to his will.

THE MASQUERADE BALL

After taking a bite from an enchanted peach, Sarah is immersed in an elaborate illusion. Jareth's Masquerade Ball features elegant gowns, cascading pearls, and mist-filled mirrors. Jareth conjures this fantastical event in an effort to distract Sarah from her quest. As she draws perilously close to the castle, she finds herself in a chamber where masked revelers dance in a dizzying whirl and light reflects off crystal-draped candelabras. The ballroom evokes beauty, grace, and enchantment, but it is merely a mirage. Once its mirrors are shattered, its occupants drift into the ether and Sarah discovers that she has lost valuable time.

A Variety of Goblins

A vast variety of goblins provide the many services required by the Goblin King. From guards to artists to caretakers, this multitude of creatures attend to Jareth's whims. Some, like the benevolent Beedleglum, know their master's storied history and possess a unique perspective on his unpredictable behavior. Others, like the castle goblins, lack any form of intelligence and cause their King unending frustration. Though varied in appearance, acumen, and aptitude, the goblins of the Labyrinth are united in their desire to serve their monarch—while avoiding his terrible wrath.

CARETAKER GOBLINS

A great many goblins serve in caretaking roles. They tend to the needs of others, providing food and clothing and cleaning up after their charges. Among these caretakers, goblin chefs are adored across the kingdom for their ability to nourish and delight. The goblin cook Weech is famous for her ability to single-handedly prepare food for an entire army. However, she prefers to work with an assistant—one who literally puts his whole heart into his dishes, before returning the organ to his chest. This unusual ingredient is said to give his meals a most delightful boost of flavor.

Cleaning goblins—not to be confused with the subterranean Cleaners—provide another useful service. They venture across battlefields and other regions where limbs might have been lost. On finding an errant body part, they place it inside a hollow, can-shaped goblin by the name of Maeliciöüs.

Cleaning goblins might also team up with the Royal Nail Clipper, tidying up after this caretaker as he clips fellow goblins' fingernails and toenails. Because the Clipper leaves behind a trail of dismembered digits, he is said to be the reason that the Labyrinth has so many three-toed goblins.

THE GOBLIN ARMY

The labyrinth is inherently dangerous, and kings have long employed soldiers for its defense. The Goblin Army is made up of multiple units, each of which utilizes a particular method of attack.

Mounted soldiers use pikes and spears to drive invaders back, bombardiers wield cannons to force retreat, and foot soldiers chase unwelcome visitors through the streets. Each platoon is unyielding in its approach. After all, the kings of the Labyrinth have never tolerated failure . . . and their soldiers wouldn't dream of disappointing them.

The goblin military has many moving parts. In addition to soldiers, the Labyrinth's kings have also employed scouts on reptilian steeds, who gallop through the maze bearing lances and flags as they scour for unwanted visitors. Target goblins are deployed during military exercises; they offer themselves as bull's-eyes, helping their comrades to practice their aim. And rear protection goblins ride backwards into battle, forming a unit that is at its most formidable while exiting a skirmish. Although goblin brigades may appear unorganized, the soldiers of the Labyrinth readily rush into battle when they hear their call to arms: "Halt, and all that!"

GOBLIN WEAPONRY

Goblin soldiers carry an assortment of weapons, from pikes to spears to spiked balls. Some are forged by blacksmith elves, while others are crafted through less traditional means. Goblins have many unconventional weapons at their disposal, including the Dream-Pick—a device that is capable of piercing dreams. Angst-Plugs are attached to a goblin, bottling up the victim's fears and causing them to explode in a fit of diffidence. And the mere swipe of a Luck-Ladle can wipe away an entire lifetime of good fortune.

While the long-footed goblins that resemble spiky-helmeted spheres are usually used soletly as cannonballs, the similarly built Fodder can function as both an offensive weapon and a teapot. Goblins' general eagerness to please, along with a respectful fear of their overlord, make them highly amenable to a life of service—regardless of what that might entail.

NIPPER STICKS

Among the goblins' more worrisome weapons are the dreaded Nipper Sticks—long, thin poles topped by aggressive toothed beings that bite everything they encounter. These fierce creatures cling to their sticks with pointed talons, leaving their jaws free to gnash on anything within reach. With sharp protruding fangs and a pole-length reach, Nipper Sticks can be highly dangerous weapons.

Because the creatures are prone to attacking their handlers, the goblins who carry them wear spiked helmets and metal shoulder plates to avoid undue injury.

GOBLIN AMUSEMENTS

Athletic pursuits offer an escape from everyday routines, and goblin athletes are respected for both their physical prowess and their bravery. Games like Lunchball require teams of identically clothed goblins to compete to be the first to eat a ball, and then discern *which* player has consumed it. In Goblin-Head Banging, contestants don poison-tipped horns with which they attempt to stab one another. The venom from these horns will cause a victim's pants to fall off. And in another curious amusement, Eled's Worm Circus showcases a troupe of highly trained worms. These creatures have been taught to stand end to end, grow to sixty feet in length, and battle their ringmaster—much to the delight of their goblin audiences!

GOBLIN SPECIALTIES

Other goblins fill unique roles within their communities. For example, politician Røem Bååbå is not only known for serving as prime minister, but also for being the host of the World's Biggest Flea. Bønüs Eventüs possesses a variety of body parts that speak incessantly. Gürtie goblins are nearly as likely to issue a fatal bite as they are to offer a cup of homemade cocoa.

While each of these types of goblins serves an individual function, all contribute to the collective curiosity of the great goblin kingdom.

ARTISTS

Goblin artists serve an important function within the Labyrinth. Their works inspire and amuse, distracting residents from their everyday toils. The performing arts scene is particularly engaging, with poets like Brêgg amassing a significant number of admirers, while actors Aprön and Gibbergeist have achieved astounding levels of fame. Popular physical artists depict scenes of death and destruction—subjects that goblins find less controversial than more lighthearted works of art. And the fashionable clothing from designers Nive and Førwke is admired throughout the kingdom. However, because the garments have such high prices and are made from fabrics that are far too heavy to wear, this pair has never sold a single design.

BANDITS AND THE GOBLIN HORDE

Particularly spirited residents of the Labyrinth might eventually leave the maze to join the bandits. These packs of creatures roam the High Hills that surround the Labyrinth, creating mischief and chaos wherever they go. Intriguingly, the infamous goblin bandit Feedle has been known to return stolen goods to his victims. He cleans the items up, attaches a poem he has written himself, and delivers his bounty to its original owners—even if he has already killed them.

The Goblin Horde gathers in a region known as the Great Howling Waste. While nobody is certain just what this horde is composed of, it is known to be watched over by three goblin keepers: Lampsöniüs, Cändlewic, and Agmöür. These vigilant guardians are so dedicated to their work that they forego sleep, food, and holidays.

THE SAGE AND HIS ASSISTANT

The aging goblin Loch is renowned for his wisdom. An accomplished mediator of disputes, he travels across the labyrinth issuing judgments on behalf of those who seek his services.

Because his pronouncements take Loch some time—in one case, a full seventy days—he occasionally finds that these quarrels resolve themselves. However, when a solution is not forthcoming, he has been known to employ the services of additional goblins to hasten the process. Loch is frequently accompanied by his usher, Ness, a diminutive goblin whose subservient nature makes him a most willing assistant.

THE CLEANERS

Deep beneath the Labyrinth's surface, a blade-lined
device speeds through the twisting stone tunnels.
This machine's spinning cleavers are operated by four
determined goblins, each of whom is tasked with removing
unwanted debris.

These goblin Cleaners are unyielding in their pursuit of cleanliness—and those unlucky enough to get in their way might find themselves sucked into the swirling skewers of their deadly apparatus.

THE JUNK LADY

This frowning goblin with weather-worn skin
lives in the Junkyard at the base of the Goblin
City. She is one of the many Junk People who
roam this clutter-strewn region, collecting
crockery, furniture, and bottles to pile atop
their deeply hunched backs. The Junk Lady uses
her treasures to distract travelers who have drawn
too near to the maze's center. She may offer a visitor
individual items from her stash or invite them into a room
filled with mementoes from their life beyond the Labyrinth.
A visit to one of these rooms can distract occupants for hours,
enabling the Goblin King to run out the clock on his victims,
trapping the Junk Lady's target within the Labyrinth forever.

THE GOBLIN CITY GATES

The Goblin City is situated just beyond the Junkyard and is guarded by two gates. A sleepy guard protects the outer archway, where a set of thick wooden doors remains unlocked. The second gate, however, is considerably more imposing—and far less likely to be breached.

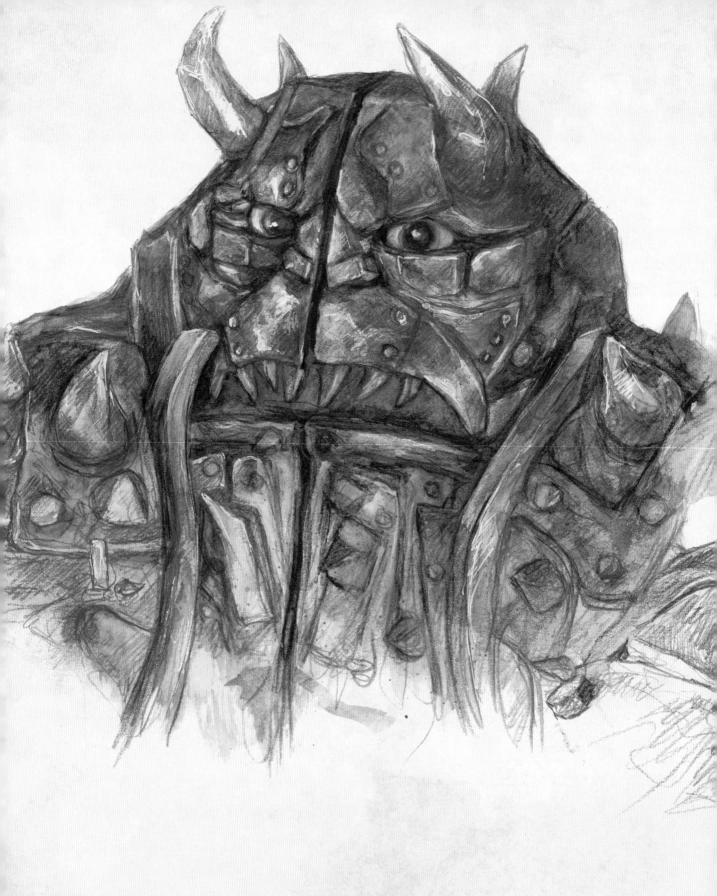

HUMONGOUS

The inner gate of the Goblin City makes up two halves of one terrible creature. When the doors close and the halves join together, they merge into the frightening form of Humongous. This massive armored guardian emerges from the gates as a fully formed metallic monster. His gaping mouth and glowing eyes strike fear into even the bravest of hearts. But Humongous is merely a machine—one controlled by a small goblin situated within Humongous's cavernous head. Once the goblin detaches Humongous from the doorway, he uses a lever to operate the machine's twin-headed axe. This formidable weapon is capable of shattering stone, spraying sparks, and destroying buildings. Once unleashed, Humongous makes for a truly terrifying adversary.

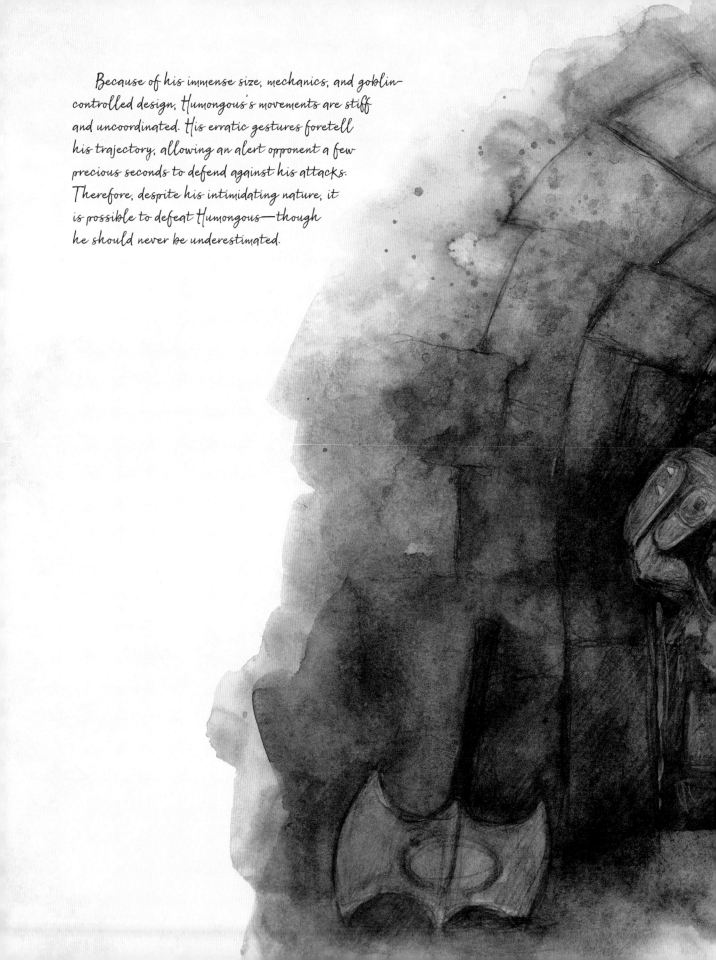

Because of his immense size, mechanics, and goblin-controlled design, Humongous's movements are stiff and uncoordinated. His erratic gestures foretell his trajectory, allowing an alert opponent a few precious seconds to defend against his attacks. Therefore, despite his intimidating nature, it is possible to defeat Humongous—though he should never be underestimated.

HOME OF THE GOBLINS

The Goblin City is an aging, run-down township that houses many of the Labyrinth's goblins. Though its rooftops are shabby and its walls falling apart, it provides a welcome respite for the countless residents who call it home.

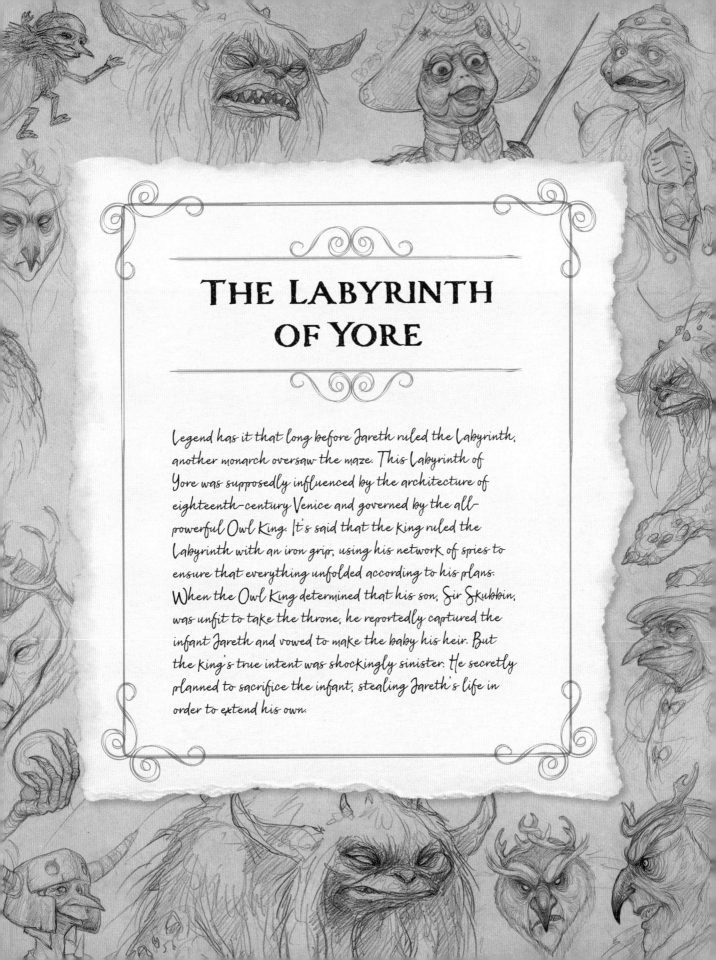

THE LABYRINTH OF YORE

Legend has it that long before Jareth ruled the Labyrinth, another monarch oversaw the maze. This Labyrinth of Yore was supposedly influenced by the architecture of eighteenth-century Venice and governed by the all-powerful Owl King. It's said that the King ruled the Labyrinth with an iron grip, using his network of spies to ensure that everything unfolded according to his plans. When the Owl King determined that his son, Sir Skubbin, was unfit to take the throne, he reportedly captured the infant Jareth and vowed to make the baby his heir. But the king's true intent was shockingly sinister. He secretly planned to sacrifice the infant, stealing Jareth's life in order to extend his own.

Some stories tell that Jareth's mother, Maria, demanded that the King return Jareth. But she was issued a challenge by the monarch: If she could successfully traverse the Labyrinth and reach its castle before the clock struck thirteen, the Owl King would hand back her son. But if she failed, Jareth would die—and Maria would become the king's slave. Determined to save her child, Maria teamed up with a trio of adventurers to fight through a goblin graveyard, cross a cluster of burning bridges, and outsmart both swamp goblins and Gondoliers—unscrupulous gondola drivers known for stealing both time and possessions. Although Maria and her friends did eventually reach the castle, she found herself unable to fully free her son. When the Owl King died, it was Jareth who became the Labyrinth's ruler—and, in a nod to his predecessor, developed the ability to transform into an owl.

The Owl King's legendary Labyrinth bore many similarities to its later incarnation under the Goblin King. Like its counterpart, the Labyrinth of Yore housed an unbending monarch, inhospitable environments, and a gaggle of curious beasts. But this fabled Labyrinth held a particular darkness—one brought about by its calculating King and his desire to reign in perpetuity. Carnivorous beasts guarded the castle, while its nursery housed a tyrannical doll that demanded impossible answers. Skyfaring prison ships sailed through the clouds and a night troll terrorized anyone who dared to cross the King. But even within this darkness, there were shining sparks of light. The conflicted knight Sir Skubbin, the gentle bloom Tangle, and the brave revolutionary Cible all longed for a world in which they controlled their destinies. It would take a chance meeting with Maria to launch each on their quest, but these adventurers would one day challenge the Owl King and discover that friendship can be an overwhelmingly powerful force.

THE OWL KING

The Owl King oversaw the Labyrinth with an unyielding will. He surrounded himself with the fiercest of allies, feeding his foes to his winged lion guard, the Featherfang, and sending his night troll, Septimus, to execute his enemies. When Maria encountered him, the Owl King was cruel, unpopular, and near the end of his natural life. But even so, anyone who dared to defy him quickly found themselves silenced.

The Owl King was said to be as cold as he was calculating. He hatched a murderous plot to extend his own life and obliterated anyone who stood in the way of his goals. He despised curiosity, declaring that kings must rule—*not wonder*. And he understood that every rule had a loophole; a fact he used to his every advantage.

BEEDLEGLUM

This gentle, kindhearted goblin has served the kings of the Labyrinth for hundreds of years. He is said to have played a vital role in the Owl King's court, gaining his master's trust and earning a coveted spot within his inner chambers. According to legend, when the infant Jareth arrived in the Labyrinth, it was Beedleglum who looked after the baby. The goblin made it his life's work to care for his charge—a duty he continued when Jareth became the Goblin King. As the years went on, the kindly Beedleglum appeased his master by caring for a new infant, Toby. He showed the baby the same compassion he extended to the young Jareth—an act that helped mollify the child and also saved the Goblin King from the chore of dealing with humans.

Beedleglum has spent a lifetime striving to create harmony—both within the castle and beyond its cobwebbed walls.

FEATHERFANG

Tales tell that in the earlier version of the Labyrinth, a massive winged lion was carved into the gates of the Owl King's chambers. This enormous beast stood on three wide paws while the fourth gripped a frighteningly sharp sword. When challenged, the Featherfang would come to life, breaking free of his door before launching himself at anyone who tried to enter his master's sanctuary. His vicious determination ensured that the castle was rarely breached. All within the King's court were well aware that if they dared to cross their ruler, they might just be fed to the Featherfang.

THE PAVEMENT

The base of the Labyrinth of Yore was reportedly comprised of ever-shifting surfaces. But one face-shaped section of stones, the Pavement, possessed a mind of its own. It offered unsolicited counsel and warned residents of the king's deepening displeasure. And when insulted, the Pavement crumbled in on itself to create a gaping hole. The Pavement also served as a visual conduit. The Owl King was said to have peered through its stones to examine what was happening within the Labyrinth. This unique vantage point gave the monarch an ongoing view of his kingdom—and turned the Pavement into an unlikely spy.

CONDOLIERS

Wild-eyed goblins with deceitful dispositions, the Condoliers were said to be among the Labyrinth of Yore's most confusing foes. They rowed lithe gondolas across the maze's many canals and bore a striking likeness to the helpful gondoliers of eighteenth-century Venice. But unlike their human counterparts, Condoliers were known for swindling passengers. As it turned out, the only place a Condolier would *never* take a traveler . . . was the very destination that individual had requested!

SEPTIMÜS

Legend has it that the Owl King's pet shadow spread terror across the Labyrinth. Septimüs's twin-horned head and sharp-toothed jaw made him a fatal assailant. And the rows of spikes across his broad back offered a degree of protection from counterattack.

Septimüs apparently existed to do the king's bidding. This night troll was similar in build to the great beast Ludo, but the creatures' resemblance ended there. While Ludo was both gentle and loyal, Septimüs was cruel and utterly uncompromising. He took pride in his role as the king's executioner and eagerly moved from one kill to the next.

SIR SKUBBIN

This aspiring bandit reputedly possessed a deeply conflicted soul. Sir Skubbin had hoped to join a bandit horde in the Great Howling Waste but was forced to abandon his dream when he found himself unable to locate the Labyrinth's elusive exit. Although it's said he rescued Maria from the clutches of a swamp goblin, it seems Sir Skubbin only did so in order to steal from her. To his great embarrassment, the knight carried a deeply shameful secret: Although he wanted to be mischievous, chaotic, and ridiculous, he was cursed with the most awful burden a goblin could carry—a noble heart.

Sir Skubbin's curse was even more humiliating on account of his lineage. As the son of the Owl King, he wanted nothing to do with his heritage. After stealing a piece of chalk from Maria, he was overwhelmed with guilt and gifted her his royal ring as a trade. And as their friendship developed, Skubbin chose to help Maria save her son's life. As the years went on, Skubbin learned to follow the desires of his heart. Reports say that he eventually became a bandit and achieved his dream of exploring the Great Howling Waste.

TANGLE

This gentle walking rosebush was said to possess wild thorns, spiky arms, and the ability to grow on command. When threatened, Tangle could elongate, extending willowy limbs to ward off attackers. Tangle was reportedly both male and female and possessed an extremely gentle heart. Tangle longed to embrace friends, but the bush's thorny branches kept everyone at arm's length.

Stories say that Tangle encouraged companions to focus on solving one problem at a time—a strategy that paid off when Tangle, Sir Skubbin, and the brave worm, Cible, joined Jareth's mother on her quest to save her child. Although the group was unable to free Jareth, they successfully thwarted the Owl King's plans to do away with the child. Years later, Jareth showed his gratitude by commanding Tangle's goblin flies to hug the gentle creature at least once every day.

GOBLIN FLIES

It's said that goblin flies were small winged creatures with goblin-like faces. Their heads were covered with colorful hats, each of which was decorated to resemble a ladybug, butterfly, or beetle. They were also known to have sharp stinging bites that caused recipients to fall into a disoriented mental state. Despite this troublesome habit, goblin flies spread joy through kind acts. When ordered to embrace Tangle, they performed their duty with cheerful smiles.

BUNDERGHAST THE INVINCIBLE AKA CIBLE

As a great goblin leader, Bunderghast the Invincible was a Labyrinth legend. The revolutionary was rumored to be as large as a castle, with a spike-covered body and a tendency to carry ale barrels wherever he went. He was prophesied to ignite a full-scale goblin rebellion, which led an eager army of aspiring rebels to hole up in a sewer and await his arrival. However, reports say that during a goblin census, an administrator inadvertently made a clerical error that transferred the name intended for the fierce goblin revolutionary to a tiny pink worm. The name of the great warrior, Bunderghast the Invincible, was thus gifted to Cible—who adopted her nickname as a shortened version of Invincible. Although she was tiny, Cible was said to have more than lived up to her title. She abhorred bullies, fought for fairness, and apparently helped Jareth's mother recover her son. Cible embraced her revolutionary role by wearing a bow, a cape, and a pirate hat. It was her fervent desire to help each of her friends make their dreams come true.

As years passed, Cible reputedly became both a hero and a legend. She took her place among the realm's many celebrated champions, each of whom braved dangers, faced hardships, and worked alongside their fellow adventurers to overcome the greatest and most perilous obstacle of all: the Labyrinth.

TITAN
BOOKS

A division of Titan Publishing Group Ltd
144 Southwark Street
London SE1 0UP
www.titanbooks.com

 Find us on Facebook: www.facebook.com/Titanbooks

Follow us on X: @titanbooks

Published by Titan Books, London, in 2022.

A CIP catalogue record for this title is available from the
British Library.

ISBN: 9781803361048

INSIGHT EDITIONS

Publisher: Raoul Goff
VP of Licensing and Partnerships: Vanessa Lopez
VP of Creative: Chrissy Kwasnik
VP of Manufacturing: Alix Nicholaeff
Editorial Director: Vicki Jaeger
Designer: Amy DeGrote
Executive Editor: Chris Prince
Assistant Editor: Harrison Tunggal
Senior Production Editor: Elaine Ou
Senior Production Manager: Greg Steffen
Senior Production Manager, Subsidiary Rights: Lina s Palma

Illustrations by Iris Compiet

ACKNOWLEDGMENTS

INSIGHT EDITIONS would like to thank everyone at the Jim
Henson Company who made this book possible, including
Lisa Henson, Brian Henson, Jim Formanek, Nicole Goldman,
Carla DellaVedova, Shannon Robles, Karen Falk, Susie Tofte,
and Debra Shapiro. We also extend our thanks to Sierra Hahn,
Allyson Gronowitz, Gavin Gronenthal, Cameron Chittock,
Simon Spurrier, Daniel Bayliss at BOOM! Studios, and the entire
team at Archaia Entertainment. Additional thanks to Brian and
Wendy Froud for all their help and inspiration, and to Toby
Froud for his wonderful foreword.

Iris Compiet would like to thank everyone who made the original
film *Labyrinth*—still a source of inspiration and daydreams—
including Brian and Wendy Froud, and everyone at the Jim
Henson Company. And finally, many thanks to the team at
Insight Editions and her husband, Bart.

S.T. Bende wishes to thank the Jim Henson Company for a
lifetime of inspiration—and for letting her get lost in their
Labyrinth! Huge thanks to Iris Compiet, Chris Prince, and the
team at Insight Editions for making this project so magical. And
orbs of gratitude to her husband and their kind little goblins, who
always say yes to adventure.

ROOTS of PEACE   REPLANTED PAPER

Insight Editions, in association with Roots of Peace, will plant two trees
for each tree used in the manufacturing of this book. Roots of Peace is
an internationally renowned humanitarian organization dedicated to
eradicating land mines worldwide and converting war-torn lands into
productive farms and wildlife habitats. Roots of Peace will plant two
million fruit and nut trees in Afghanistan and provide farmers there with
the skills and support necessary for sustainable land use.

Manufactured in China by Insight Editions

10 9 8 7 6 5 4 3